Edwin Goadby

Shakespeare's Time

A Lecture Delivered at the York Institute, November 5, 1878

Edwin Goadby

Shakespeare's Time
A Lecture Delivered at the York Institute, November 5, 1878

ISBN/EAN: 9783337063856

Printed in Europe, USA, Canada, Australia, Japan

Cover: Foto ©Thomas Meinert / pixelio.de

More available books at **www.hansebooks.com**

SHAKESPEARE'S TIME:

A LECTURE

DELIVERED AT THE YORK INSTITUTE,

NOVEMBER 5, 1878;

WITH

"A PILGRIMAGE
TO STRATFORD-ON-AVON,"

Reprinted from SHARPE'S LONDON MAGAZINE.

BY

EDWIN GOADBY,

EDITOR OF THE "YORK DAILY HERALD."

———————◆———————

LONDON:
ARTHUR H. MOXON, 12, TAVISTOCK ST., COVENT GARDEN.
YORK:
JOHN SAMPSON.

PRICE SIXPENCE.

PREFACE.

THE following lecture was not written with a view to its publication, nor would the success which attended its delivery have inclined me to print it, had it not been a first-thought with others and a second-thought with myself, that it might usefully contribute to a clearer popular understanding of the time in which Shakespeare lived and wrote. I am not vain enough to imagine that thoughtful and cultivated persons will find much in the paper that is either fresh in matter or novel in present-ment; but, nevertheless, there may be something to interest them in a modest contribution to the study of one of England's greatest men, and one of the most creative periods in her history. An account of a visit I made to Stratford-on-Avon, in 1859, has been re-printed and added at the suggestion of a friend, who is a native of the place, and whose kindly criticisms induced me to disentomb the sketch for his perusal. It may, perhaps, serve to give a certain amount of completeness, as well as of contrast, to the picture I have attempted.

16, Bootham, York.

Triumph, my Britain, thou has one to show,
To whom all scenes of Europe homage owe.
He was not of an age, but for all time!
BEN JONSON.

SHAKESPEARE'S TIME.

THE heritage a great man leaves the world is to force it to explain him. So says the German philosopher, Hegel; and it would seem that the world will never weary of explaining William Shakespeare. The characters of common mortals can be written by a skilful penman in the space covered by a shilling; but the great dead provoke so much thought in others that to the making of books upon them there is no end, and in the reading of many of them there is much weariness of the flesh. They lie about like the moraines and moving glaciers which conceal from us for a time some entrancing Jungfrau, pinnacled in solitary splendour. I believe I am not exceeding the truth when I say that a thousand books have been written about Shakespeare, and that there are nearly as many explanations—French, German, Italian, American, and English. If the natives of Central Africa should ever have a literature of their own, they will give us another theory of Shakespeare, with especial reference to Othello, the Moor of Venice. These explanations of great men have reference sometimes to the stars under which they were born, to their nurses and playmates, to their bumps and biliary ducts, to their familiarity with good and evil spirits, and to their enormous and unacknowledged appropriation of the oral and written works of others. I have no such explanation to give concerning Shakespeare. I doubt my own capacity to explain him at all. It is my intention to depict the time in which he lived, and to let the time assist in explaining the man. This may seem a paltry, evasive method, very like the Tartar's swallowing of the prescription instead of the medicine; but it is next to impossible to understand any great man until you have looked all round him, held converse with his contemporaries, and walked by his side amidst the familiar scenes of his every-day life. It has been said of Shakespeare, however, that he owed very little to his contemporaries or to the book-learning of his time. Hume says he was " without any instruction either

from the world or from books." But this is a transcendental
view of the matter, in direct conflict with fact. Poetical genius
clothes, transforms, and vivifies, but it borrows much of its raw
material; and even when it revolts against the age in which it
lives, it owes to it the spring of disgust which sends it back
to classic times, or forward to some better era.

In reality, Shakespeare's genius owed more to external circum-
stances than is usual with great men. The love of the drama
was in existence before he ministered unto it. There were
eminent dramatists before he had penned a line. Most of his
plays were founded upon novels, legends, and histories current in
his day. They are full of allusions to contemporary events,
manners, customs, and modes of thought. His classic heroes
are quite as familiar with English as with Greek and Roman
customs. The whole bent of his mind towards the stage was
due to local and general influences; his style was, to a great
extent, moulded upon the best contemporary writings; his plays
are full of satires upon the men and women of his day; and
many of his characters are as Elizabethan as are their ceremonies,
their articles of dress and food, their phrases and their weapons.
" Trinculo and Stephano," says Mr. G. W. Thornbury, " were
men to be met any day in St. Paul's, their clothes long since dry
from the surges of the Bermoothes, and their skins quite healed
from the lashes of the boatswain; quibbling Speed and Lance
and his dog might have lived at Charlecote; Robin, Simple, and
Rugby have been seen running up Bucklersbury; Malvolio gaping
at the prisoners looking out of the grating at Ludgate; and
Lancelot, tricksome, at Bartholomew's Fair, intent on tawdry
ribbons as a present for the sprightly Maria, Sir Toby Belch's
widow, who is expectantly waiting at a roast-pig stall. Sir
Toby Belch, in his disreputable boots, ' good enough for drinking
in,' and Sir John Falstaff, wittiest of sinners, might, we dare
venture to say, have been found quaffing burnt sack together on
the snug bench of some ale-house at Ilogsden. Abhorson and
Bernardine were common inmates of the Counter, with Shoe-Tie,
the great traveller, and Half-can who stabbed Pots. Costard
and Bottom might have been rustics of Stafford, and Sir
Nathaniel and Sir Oliver Martext hedge-priests not a mile from
Warwick. In the *Tempest* we find him talking of the ' Dead
Indian ' and such penny shows as were to be seen any day in
Fleet Street or the Strand; the serenades in the *Two Gentlemen
of Verona* and *Cymbeline* were strains heard at a hundred terrace
windows any bright morning of the Elizabethan year; the porter

in *Macbeth* is just such a porter as whipped out Lance's dog when he misbehaved himself in the Duke's chamber; Slender brags of his feats at bear-baiting, and took Saccarson by the chain; *Henry VI.* is full of allusions drawn from the Paris garden, adjoining Shakespeare's theatre; Sir Andrew Ague-Cheek uses the phrases of Saviolo and the fencing masters of the day; Pistol mouths scraps of plays just as the play-going bullies used at the Three Cranes in the Vintry, or the Devil in Fleet Street; Dr. Caius is the French physician of the day, just as Sir Armado is the conventional Spaniard, Shylock the conventional Jew, and Evans the conventional Welshman. Mother Pratt of Brentford is a white witch, the mere fortune-teller of the age, just as the *Macbeth* spirits are beings of the same family elevated into poetry, but still working with the vulgar machinery of such witches as Hopkins gave over to the flames, or James I. denounced; Autolycus, first a pedlar and then a cutpurse, might have stood in a London pillory with Nym and Bardolph, who were stealers of clocks at taverns; the Windsor Fairies, like those of the *Midsummer Night*, had not yet fled at the first shriek of the railway whistle, and were still visible to the believing." Any obscure allusion, any misuse of a word, any snatch of a song, is to be regarded as contemporary history, in a fragmentary form, which would make his plays pointed to an audience where they are but dull to us. But, amongst these contemporary sketches and characters, were men of no age who have been made by him men for all time. His genius breathed upon them, and Hamlet, Lear, Othello, and Timon are immortal; the possessions of the human race, and not the creatures of a single age.

Europe was a strange medley in Shakespeare's time—that is, from 1564 to 1616. In the East, the Turk was supreme, ruling from Constantinople to Buda-Pesth, from Podolia to the Morea; and his character, as Shakespeare judged him, may be found in *King Lear*, where he is described as "false of heart, light of ear, bloody of hand; hog in sloth, fox in stealth, wolf in greediness, dog in madness, lion in prey," which is pretty much what he remains to the present day, though more veneered with Western civilization. Russia was just coming into prominence, and English merchants were trading there. Ivan the Terrible, the first Russian who had assumed the title of Tsar, was bold enough to offer his hand in marriage to Queen Elizabeth. The German Empire stretched from the Baltic to the Adriatic, and divided with Spain the supreme control of the Continent; Italy was a geographical expression; Sweden and Norway had been recently Protestantised; the Dutch Republic was coming into being; and France, although relieved from the burden of English power, groaned alike under Spanish domination and Papal intrigue. The little Republic of Venice was beginning to languish and lose its commerce and its Greek Islands. It lost Cyprus in 1573, when Shakespeare was nine years old, and had been two years at Stratford Free Grammar School. His Othello, as you know, was Governor of Cyprus, and in the play tidings arrive that the Turk, "with a most mighty preparation, makes for Cyprus;" and then, later, when the scene of the play is changed from Venice to Cyprus itself, every man is commanded "to put himself into triumph," because news had come "importing the mere (or entire) perdition of the Turkish Fleet." The play was written in 1604, when the Turks were in full possession of the island. Continuing our survey, we may note that Scotland was tied to the fortunes of the beautiful and passionate Mary, thundered at by Knox, divided and tempted by France, but finally won over to Calvin and the Reformation. Ireland was the despair of everybody, of the Irish no less than the English. The latter were settled in the Counties of Dublin, Meath, Louth, and Kildare, comprising what was called the English Pale, and they took care to shave the upper lip, so as not to be mistaken for the "wild Irish," who dwelt outside the Pale. Wales was improving under justices, nominated by the Lord Chancellor, who made short work of its rebels. And what of England? She had ceased, in the sense of ownership, to be a Continental Power; but she was always interfering, impelled by religious or dynastic sympathies, in Continental politics; supporting the Reformers in France and the Low Countries, braving the Pope, defying the Spaniards; and sending forth her Drakes and Frobishers, her Raleighs and Gilberts, to found new colonies, to discover new continents and islands, and to pour into the lap of trade the spoils of the Indies and the products of the New World.

Historians usually make too much of dynastic troubles and court intrigues; of battles and sieges, and the larger movements of the time. I shall reverse this method, and pay less attention to the history of the time, as recorded in ordinary books, than to the life and people of the time, and their customary doings and pursuits. Though I cannot pass over in silence the great struggle between the Popes and the kingly and popular power, I must leave you to trace it out for yourselves at leisure, for time would fail me to recount its religious and political beginnings, the revolts it occasioned, the intrigues it developed, the national divisions it accentuated, the massacres which marked its course ; the struggles of Henry VIII., the severities of Thomas Cromwell, the Protector ; the restoration of Popery under Queen Mary ; the persecutions of the martyrs ; the establishment of Protestantism under Queen Elizabeth ; the changes she made in the Church ; her quarrel with Spain ; and the destruction of that tremendous Armada which was sent to conquer and wipe out England, in the interests of Rome, but which ended in the annihilation of Spain as a leading power in Europe. I cannot enter into the disputes as to the lovers, the intrigues, or the death of Mary Queen of Scots. I must be forgiven if I do not describe the invasion of these islands by the Jesuits, and the plots in which they delighted ; or the rebellions against Elizabeth, and the fate of some of her favourites. I wish to bring you face to face with the English people, unconquered alike by Pope or Spaniard. I desire to make you familiar with the old land of which Shakespeare says, in *King John :*

> This England never did, nor never shall,
> Lie at the proud foot of a conqueror.

Let us take a bird's eye view of the land itself. Its chief physical aspects were much the same as now, but vast tracts were not under cultivation. There were fens and marshes in Lancashire as well as in Lincolnshire ; woods of oak, hazel, and beech covered extensive districts now turned over by the plough or thickly set with houses and factory chimneys. The woods were decaying, however, as Harrison, an old writer, remarks, and no wonder, seeing that coal, though in use here and there, was considered a nuisance; that wood was the principal fuel; and that only occasionally were the poor people ingenious enough to plaster their houses and walls with cow-dung in the summer, to peel it off and use it for fuel in the winter—a practice continued in some parts to the middle half of last century, and borrowed, I suspect, from the Turks, through information afforded by Crusaders. These wild open lands, half wood, half common, were the resort of thousands of gypsies, who then called themselves Egyptians, and were unmistakably Indian in colour, dress, and language. They were half bandits; and as they moved about mostly by night, the common people called them *moonmen.* The laws against them were severe, for it was a felony to be found consorting with "roguish Egyptians." I have found many entries of fines for this offence in unpublished contemporary records. The Peak of Derbyshire, as we gather from Ben Jonson, was a place where they frequently met, at periodic intervals. Travelling was, of course, terribly insecure—the roads unfenced, unditched, full of holes and ruts, and forcing travellers to have teams of four and six horses to convey their wagons. Even then they were sometimes stuck fast, and bullock-teams had to be borrowed from friendly farmers by the roadside. So far as any general idea prevailed in the construction of the roads, they were made on the concave system, and not on the convex, as now; that is, they were lower in the middle than at the sides, the idea being that rain would repair the roads by washing the dirt into the middle. I have in my possession a black letter tract, in which the writer proposes a new method of mending roads, by laying down frames of wood and wattled hurdles, filling up the spaces and covering them over with stones, brick, iron-ore, slag, and rubbish. He provided for under-drainage in this fashion, and he thought so well of the plan that he brought it before King James, with many pretty diagrams and a poetical preface. I mention this to show the primitive ideas which prevailed.

Goods were carried about in heavy stage-wagons, costing fifteen pence per ton per mile. Most travellers preferred to go on horseback to running risks in heavy vehicles, and they were frequently lost on the way, as sometimes happened between York and Doncaster. The coach was just coming into use, strong built for country travel, and for show in London somewhat dainty. When the latter kind was first introduced by the wealthy, Taylor, the water-poet, says: "Some said it was a great crab-shell, brought out of China, and some imagined it to be one of the Pagan temples in which the cannibals adored the devil." So common had these fantastic private coaches become—none were on hire, even in London, before 1630—that, in 1601, a Puritanic Lord endeavoured to obtain the sanction of Parliament for an Act—" to restrain the excessive and superfluous use of coaches in this realm." But his own coach was upset on the second reading. Off the main roads pack-horses were used, as can still be gathered from public-house signs, and they were very common in Yorkshire, moving about in long strings, with poor passengers riding between their paniers. North of York and west of Exeter there were no stage wagons at all. There was no regular postal service in Elizabeth's time, and all letters were transmitted by mounted messengers, the cost including the wages of the man and the keep of his horse. James I. introduced the first regular postal system. Naturally, when there was so much heavy traffic, the roadside hostelries were immense places, often able to accommodate three hundred guests and their horses and servants. They were like little villages in otherwise solitary wastes. Here you would meet a company of strolling players, wearing the costumes of their characters, in which they frequently travelled ; a member of Parliament on the jog to London; a justice of the peace and a *posse* of constables in hot pursuit of a thief ; a fashionable highwayman, well known to ostlers and landlords, and getting news from them of empty and well-filled purses; a poor scholar bound for Cambridge or Oxford, his cob and himself a compound of leanness and learning; a grand country gentleman, with a whole retinue of mounted and running servants ; and scores of foot-passengers ever on the move, paying a penny a night for'their beds; the needy suitor on his way to the Chancery Court at York, or with stern face intent on battling with the rich lawyers in Westminster Hall ; pedlars, tinkers, broken-down soldiers, limping home from the Low Countries ; ear-ringed sailors full of yarns about the Indies and the Turks ; the ballad-singer on his way to the nearest fair ; and the cunning gamester, with his cards and his dice, who would cheat you at tables in the tap-room, beat you at bowls in the bowling alley, and rob you in the inn-yard, at dusk, before you could draw your sword or cock your pistol.

The population of England at this time was much smaller than we might expect to find it. It was a little over five millions when a census was taken at the time of the Armada. That is, it was equal to the present united population of London, Liverpool, Manchester, Salford, Birmingham, and Leeds. Why it was not larger is a considerable problem, because there is good evidence to show that before the Black Death of 1348-9 there were quite as many people in England as during Elizabeth's reign. By the aid of some manuscripts in the Minster Library, Mr. Seebohm has examined the question, and the curious may find his arguments and conclusions in the second volume of the *Fortnightly Review*. It may be taken as proved that the Black Death and the Sweating Sickness of 1551 had taken off fully half of the population, saying nothing as to the drain of land and naval campaigns. A check had also arisen to that Flemish or Dutch immigration which affected the whole of the east coast of England. Mr. Froude thinks that the decaying towns, of which we hear in the early part of Elizabeth's reign, were due to the greater security of life and property, which induced the people to

leave the walled towns and settle in the villages, there to carry
on their trade. This may be a partial explanation, but it must
be supplemented by the causes I have already mentioned. In
the case of this city, then famous for its coverlets, it is recorded
that it was once well inhabited, but in Edward VI.'s time was
much reduced, the cause being " the decay of that woollen manu-
facture by which a great number of the inhabitants of the said
city and suburbs, and other places in the county of York, had
formerly been daily set on work." It is not improbable that the
bad cloth made in England had something to do with this decay
of trade. " As we have the best wools in the world," says an
old writer, " so we ought to have the best cloth ; but," he adds,
" there is more false cloth and woollen made in this realm than
in all Europe besides. All countries be now trying to make their
own cloth in consequence." The population of York, estimated
at 30,000 prior to the Black Death, was 11,000 in 1377, and not
much more in the latter part of the sixteenth century. Leeds
contained a population of about 7,000. I may mention here that
the surname of Walker, very common in Yorkshire, is of Flemish
origin. A walker was a man who worked at the walche (walke)
or fulling mill ; and in the earlier Manchester directories all the
fullers, or cloth-dressers, were called *walkers*. The city of London had a population of about 100,000. Bristol, the second
English port—for Liverpool could only boast of 4,000 people—
contained about 30,000 souls, and was a rich, thriving city, noted
for its West Indian trade. Norwich was the chief manufacturing
centre in the kingdom, and had been enriched by successive emi-
grations of persecuted Flemish Protestants, who brought with
them the knowledge of new arts and industries. Its population
had been 50,000 prior to the Black Death, but was now about
29,000. Its cloths, fustians, and silks were known all over England. Manchester, an ill-built place of less than 6,000 people,
was commencing to work up cotton from Cyprus and Smyrna
in imitation of woollen goods. Its *coatings*, or cottons, were just
beginning to win a name. Birmingham was a town of 4,000,
Sheffield of 2,000—our steel goods were then imported ; and iron
and glass had begun to be manufactured at Newcastle. Coventry manufactured blue thread, Worcester salt, Taunton broad-
cloth, Buckingham lace, Fulham tapestry, Sandwich baizes; and
Yarmouth, no longer importing its salt herrings from Iceland,
was, under Flemish tuition, beginning that trade which has since
made it famous. Bath and Cheltenham were noted places ; Plymouth a quaint seaport ; and the men of Devon, next to the men

of Middlesex, were the most daring, the most loyal, the most complete Englishmen of the day, either as soldiers, sailors, courtiers, or statesmen.

It is impossible I can give you a description of particular towns, but you may fairly ask of me what was their general appearance. The larger ones were surrounded by walls, and dominated by castles and donjon-keeps. For the most part the houses were common, built of timber where it was plentiful, of timber and stone where both were abundant, with overhanging upper storeys; the outside walls plastered over with cement, sometimes, as Harrison notes, of "delectable whitenesse." Glass windows were just beginning to replace windows of lattice-work, made of wicker or of "rifts of oak, checker-wise." Fire-places and chimneys were absent from the houses of the poor, even in towns, and the roofs were made of reeds, not of straw-thatch, as in later times. Rushes were used to cover the earthen floors of the lower rooms. So great, indeed, was the contrast between the style of the buildings and the living of the people that a Spaniard said of them—"These English have their houses made of sticks and dirt, but they fare commonlie as well as the King." The houses of the better class in the towns had parapetted fronts, with quaint gable ends, and were enclosed by walls. The rooms were wainscotted, not with English but with Danish oak; the staircases were massive and carved; the furniture substantial and costly. Glass windows were so common in the houses of the rich that Lord Bacon complained that they were now "so full of glass that we cannot tell where to come to be out of the sun or the cold." Stoves were making their appearance in merchants' houses and family mansions. In the country, the peasants' houses were always of one storey, and consisted of two rooms. The farm houses were larger and more substantial, though generally built of timber. The same may be said of the manor-houses, in which the smaller country gentlemen resided, with offices at the back for servants. Three things, however, had been marvellously altered in Harrison's time; he says: first, "the multitude of chimneys lately erected," whereas formerly "ech one made his fire against the reredosse in the hall, where he dined and dressed his meat;" secondly, the "great amendment of lodging," in the substitution of feather-beds and pillows for straw pallets and wooden bolsters; and, thirdly, "the exchange of vessell, as of treene platters into pewter, and wodden spoones into silver or tin." The mansions of the nobles and barons were built in several styles, from the old castle of stone, of which there are several fine samples intact in Durham, able to resist falcon, culverin, or cannon, to the red-brick or terra-cotta house, more especially associated with the Elizabethan period—a compound of the Italian orders, with reminiscences of the Pointed style. Numbers of delightful buildings were constructed in the period— buildings pleasant to look at and to dwell in, suggesting a transition from feudal dominance to domestic comfort, from sieges and civil wars to security and freedom; buildings with fretted fronts and quadrangular courtyards, with picturesque gables and chimneys, with jutting oriels and castellated gate- ways ; buildings with Italian gardens about them, with shady walks and bowling alleys, and brilliant aviaries, and pleasant summer-houses, and plashing fountains—gardens that suggested to Lord Bacon that it was God Almighty who planted the first of them—gardens which Lancham said, referring to Kenilworth, were " not so good as Paradise for want of the fair rivers, yet better a great deal for the lack of so unhappy a tree." Some of these mansions, as Haddon Hall in Derbyshire, Hunsdon House in Herts., Holland House in Kensington, Knowle in Kent, Longleat in Wiltshire, Wollaton Hall in Nottinghamshire, are still standing, or have passed into decay in living memory. Heslington Hall, near York, is a fair specimen of restored Eliza- bethan architecture.

It would occupy me too long to describe the interiors of these commodious mansions, their common halls and chapels, their ball-rooms and chambers, their coats of mail and tapestries, and their costly plate and works of art. The age was growing in luxury, despoiling the world, and living a bright unburdened life. The ladies not averse to household duties, clever in the dairy, dexterous with the needle, accomplished on the lute, the viol, and the virginal (a kind of piano) : the gentlemen hunting with hawk and hound, skilled with bow and lance, fond of bowls, not too religious for cards, and able to talk Latin and Greek with the ladies, or cap verses and stories with the jester. Everybody rose early and fasted until dinner-time, which was at half-past ten in the country, and about noon in the towns. Beverages or " nuntions " were sometimes taken after dinner, with dessert and a nap in " mine orchard "—in remote country districts refresh- ment between breakfast and dinner is still called nuntion; but the rule was for two meals a day—dinner and supper. The last meal was lingered over, beginning at five and frequently lasting until nine p.m. It was after the heavier part of the eating was over—they had fine appetites in those days—that the fool used to make his appearance to divert the household. Touchstone, in *As You Like It*, was evidently a portrait of the domestic clown, taken from the life. " Poor Yorick," in *Hamlet*, was one of these fellows " of infinite jest." But the custom was dying out, because it was not easy to find men clever enough to play the part. Shakespeare alludes to this discontinuance in *As You Like It*, where it is said, " since the little wit that fools have was silenced, the little foolery that wise men have makes the greater show." When foolery went out there was more elaboration in eating and drinking. Tea and coffee not being in use—coffee and teetotalism both came from Turkey, the only good things that ever did, long after Shakespeare was dead (1652)—ale, and small beer, with wines of various kinds, were taken at all meals. The common wine was sack, or sherry, from Spain, Galicia, or the Canaries, into which, if at all raw, sugar was freely stirred. Hence Sir John Falstaff's saying—" If sack and sugar be a fault, God help the wicked !" Hence, too, the discoloured teeth so common during this period. For dinner the customary fare was from four to six dishes, of divers kinds. Justice Shallow's order, when he invites Falstaff, is " Some pigeons, Davy; a couple of short-legged hens; a joint of mutton, and any pretty little tiny kickshaws, tell William Cook." The common people had but two courses; a practice of which our meat and pudding are an un-recognised " survival." Falstaff's supper at the Boar's Head, in Eastcheap, was the supper of a tippler. Here was his bill : " Item, a capon, 2s. 2d. ; item, sauce, 4d. ; item, sack, two gallons, 5s. 8d. ; item, anchovies and sack after supper, 2s. 6d. ; item, bread, *ob;*" whereat Prince Henry exclaims, " O monstrous ! but one halfpenny worth of bread to this intolerable deal of sack." The best sack was not two shillings a gallon, so Falstaff was imposed upon. Ale was 1d. per gallon, and "small ale," or beer, $\frac{1}{2}$d. a gallon.

The thirstiness of the English people at that time was pro-verbial. Iago says the English " are most potent in potting;" nor is it to be wondered at when we remember how largely salt provisions entered into their ordinary diet. The farmer always had his flitches of bacon and flitches of salt mutton on hand, in addition to salt-beef and barreled-herrings from Yarmouth. In all good houses there was an imposing array of salting tubs for preserving meat. The art of stall-feeding was almost unknown to the farmers and graziers, and fresh meat, if procurable in the winter, was very lean. It was from a halfpenny to a penny a pound, equal to about one penny or the two pence of our money.

Fresh fish was the luxury of the rich, either obtained from the ponds on their estates, or carried from the nearest ports by post-horses. Fish, in the shape of salted herrings and salt-cod, was a common article of food amongst the working classes; and when they began to obtain fresh meat in the place of it, or to live upon bread and cheese, fish was commanded to be eaten by Act of Parliament, on Fridays and Saturdays, and partially on Wednesdays, not as a religious observance, but to encourage the English fishing trade. Rye and barley bread was eaten by the poor, with the frequent addition of ground beans and peas, for wheat was sometimes three pounds a quarter—equal to about six pounds of our money. The price of bread and beer was regulated by local assize officers. A learned physician of Buxton, in Derbyshire, gives an account of the various forms of bread: " Bred of dyvers graines, of divers forms, in divers places be used. Some in form of manchet, used of the gentility; some of great loafs, as is usual amongst yeomanry ; some between both, as with the franklins ; some in form of cakes, as at weddings ; some rond of hogs, as at upsittings; some simnels, cracknels, as in the Lent ; some in brode cakes, as the oten cakes in Lendall, on yrons; some on slate stones, as in the high peke; some in frying pans, as in Darbyshire; some between yrons and wapons ; some in rond cakes, as bysket for the ships. But these and all others the mayne bread of York excelleth, for that it is of the finest flour of the wheate, well-tempered, best baked, a patterne of all others the fineste."

Life in the towns was of a very jog-trot kind, except when the town happened to be the county town and the neighbouring nobles and squires came in for the season—London was a long way off in those days—with their numerous servants in blue cloth, their Irish cobs and crab-shell coaches, and their fine foreign manners; when there were balls, civic feasts, cock-fights, bear-baitings, archery-contests, and merry-makings of all descriptions, including the performance of miracle-plays and dramas. The miracle-plays were continued in ancient places like Coventry, Chester, and probably York, long after they had served their original purpose, and the chief actors were members of the various trade-guilds, who vied with each other in dress and dramatic talent. Here are a few titles of some of the miracle-plays performed in Shakespeare's youth at Chester. He would most likely see similar plays at Coventry :

Of the Creation of the Heavens, of Angels, and of Infernal Spirits.
By the Tanners.
On Noah's Deluge. By the Water-Drawers of the Dee.
On the Slaying of the Innocents. By the Goldsmiths.
On the Supper of our Lord. By the Bakers.
On the Descent of Christ into Hell. By the Cooks.

And so on. No irreverence was meant and none was felt.
Plays were performed by strolling companies in nearly all the
corporate towns, and generally on the Sunday, as provided by
Act of Parliament, because there should be no interference with
the bear-baitings common on the Thursday. The Guildhall was
generally arranged for the entertainments, and, for the most
part, they were paid for, in a lump sum, out of the town-
moneys. A mayor, wishing to make himself popular, would hire
a company of players, send round the crier, and gather a
crowded house, we may be sure. The hint may be of service
for future Lord Mayors of York. It is known for a certainty
that there were several visits of players to Stratford-on-Avon
during Shakespeare's youth. He was probably present at the
Kenilworth revels and pageants in 1575, when Elizabeth was
grandly entertained there, and he was in his eleventh year.
Captain Cox and a Coventry troupe performed there the Mas-
sacre of the Danes by the English on St. Bride's Night,
A.D. 1012.

Another town amusement was the practice of archery. Every
town had its two butts, by royal order, for the training of young
men in the English bow—"a most honest pastime in peace,"
says Roger Ascham, "a most sure weapon in warre." The
bow was of yew, ash, or elm, three fingers thick and seven
feet long. The arrows of ash—the heavier ones for use at two
hundred and fifty yards, the lighter ones for distances beyond
that. In length, from two-and-a-half feet to four feet. It
would take a very strong arm and wrist to send the heavy
arrow two hundred and fifty yards, and no man could do
it at the present time without long training. The power to do
so had failed in our later French wars, for the enemy ridiculed
our archers as their arrows fell short. The Bowyers and
Fletchers of to-day are the descendants of the bow and arrow
makers of the ages before guns and rifles. The standing army
of Elizabeth's time was not large, but every male was trained
for a soldier, and there were a million men ready to serve in case
of invasion, though only one hundred thousand were under arms
when the Spaniards were expected. Most persons habitually went
about armed, and even discreet magistrates and rotund bur-

B

gesses carried the dagger in their belts. Schools for teaching
fencing became so notorious, indeed, that they had to be re-
strained, limited to the cities, and placed under the control of
the governors. Duels and constant acts of violence were the
result of this free use of swords, daggers, hangers, and pistols.
It was true in this matter, as in others, as Falstaff puts it : " It
was always yet the trick of our English, if they have a good
thing, to make it too common." The country amusements
chiefly consisted in the due celebration of all the feasts, in
wakes and fairs, in Maypole games, and in the finding of all
sorts of excuses to drink ale, in the churchyard or on the village
green. For example, there were Whitsuntide-ales, Leet-ales,
Lamb-ales, Bride-ales, Clerk-ales, and Church-ales.

It was always possible to tell a man's class by his dress.
The general costume, then as now, was lighter than that worn
by the Germans and the Dutch. It was modelled upon French
and Italian fashions. The male costume consisted of a close jer-
kin, or waistcoat, often reversible ; a doublet, long-breasted and
padded, sometimes peaked in front like a stomacher ; hose, or
trousers, puffed out over the thighs, known as trunk-hose ; a
short coat over all ; a flat cap, a ruff round the neck, a rapier
strapped to the waist, long stockings, and shoes of various sizes
and colours. This was the typical fashion, but it was much
altered in detail. The apprentices were compelled by statute to
wear round woollen caps, " plain statute caps," as Shakespeare
calls them ; as were all persons not of high station. Their
doublets were to be made of canvas, fustian, leather, or cloth,
without ornaments ; their stockings and hose (the latter title
was afterwards limited to stockings) of white, blue, or russet ;
their overcoats, in place of the short cloak, of cloth, cotton, or
baize ; their shoes of unpinked English hide, their girdles of
leather, their ruffs plain, and their only weapon the knife. The
burgher, or citizen, displayed more ruff round the neck, and in-
dulged in gayer-coloured doublets. His coat or cloak was
usually of brown cloth. Satin sleeves and doublets, with scarlet
cloaks and gowns, were marks of Aldermanic dignity. Lawyers
wore a loose black gown and a tight-fitting coif or cap. Indeed, black cloth was wholly confined to law and divinity. The
yeoman dressed in home-spun russet in the summer, in frieze in
the winter ; the country gentleman in a brown or blue coat, with
a plain doublet, and no feather in his cap ; the rustic in grey
cloth ; the shepherd in a russet jacket, with red sleeves, and a
blue cap. As for the dandies, they affected silk and satin mate-

rials, padded or wired out their hose, covered their cloaks with lace, clothed their legs with silk stockings of various colours, feathered their hats, gilded their rapiers, and coloured their ruffs with tinted starches. Their cloaks and rapiers grew so long that Elizabeth placed two officers at the corners of the principal London streets to cut them down to decency. Beards, too, denoted a man's class. The formally-cut beard denoted the justice and the judge; the spear or dagger-shaped beard, the soldier; the dainty small beard, the wit; the bristly beard, the country clown. Ear-rings were not uncommon amongst the more extravagant young men about town, nor the long ringlets which became the mark of the Royalists in later times. One of the orders issued by Burleigh, as Chancellor of Cambridge University, was, that " no scholar do wear any long locks of hair upon his head, but that he be polled, after the manner of the gravest scholars, under pain of six shillings and eightpence."

I feel myself quite unable to do justice to the subject of ladies' costumes, to their stomachers, ruffs, and hats, to their kirtles and farthingales, to their partlets and tire-valiants, to their cauls and minevers, their chopines and supertasses. The vanity of these dear creatures was beyond belief. They painted their faces, dyed their hair, wore " the golden tresses of the dead," as Shakespeare says in one of his sonnets, to imitate the Queen's reddish locks; they steeped themselves in perfume, covered themselves in pearls and Venice gold, and made the sweetest of private confessions to the dainty Venice mirrors they carried at their girdles. Gentlemen wore their ladies' gloves in their hats, and the ladies themselves were proud to be so honoured. Now, the fashion is for the ladies to be as much like the gentlemen as possible; then, it was the gentlemen who were scarcely to be distinguished from the ladies. But there were still the ruff and the farthingale to indicate the difference, as there are now the smooth face and the back hair. I hear what Stubbs, the Puritan, says about ladies' ruffs: " One arch or pillar wherewith the devil's kingdom of great ruffs, is under-propped is a certain kind of liquid matter which they call starche, wherein the devil hath learned them to wash and die their ruffs, which being dry, will stand stiff and inflexible about their necks. And this starch they make of divers substances—all colours and hues, of white, red, blue, purple, and the like." Another easily distinguishing mark was the long sleeve, whose ends trailed on the ground, and were cast over the shoulder, as Stubbs irreverently says, " like cow's-tails." The ladies could shoot deer as well as practice that other kind of archery mentioned in *Romeo and Juliet*, where we read :

> Alas poor Romeo he is already dead ; stabbed with a white wench's black eye; shot thorough the ear with a love-song; the very pin of his heart cleft with the blind bow-boy's butt-shaft.

But they were not insipid beauties, of whom Pope might have written some of his Epistles. To lovers like Biron, in *Love's Labour Lost*, they were

> —— the books, the arts, the academes,
> That show, contain, and nourish all the world.

They were able to speak several languages ; they could retort upon you with a passage from Plato, or one of Shakespeare's "sugared sonnets," as Meres calls them ; and, above all, they could "parley Euphuism"—an affected style of antithesis and alliteration, named after Lily's *Euphues*, and of which Shakespeare makes more than an occasional use in his plays. The Queen set them a good example in these respects, for she prided herself upon her literary tastes and her linguistic skill. She also wrote some creditable poems and translations. Her courtiers were equally cultivated. Indeed, her Court was the most learned and polite in Europe, as it was the most magnificent in dress and ceremonial. The Queen's Palaces at Greenwich, Richmond, and Hampton Court were the wonder of foreign ambassadors; and I doubt if her royal progresses, her tournaments, revels, and pageants were ever surpassed. The nobles complained that they were impoverished by them, but the poor delighted in them, and they had much to do with the Queen's unbounded popularity. Spenser and Shakespeare were immensely indebted to these splendid displays for that warmth and picturesqueness of imagination which lend such a charm to their works. They undoubtedly fostered that love for spectacular display which found in the drama its legitimate gratification.

The court fashions were borrowed from France and Venice. The Duke of York, in *Richard II.*, complains of the King being so engrossed with the

> Report of fashions in proud Italy,
> Whose manners still our tardy apish nation
> Limps after, in base imitation.

It was from Venice, also, came the external polish, the dazzling magnificence, and the intellectual vivacity of the time. It was the great centre of polite learning and manners. Of the ten thousand books issued in Europe between 1470 and 1500, some two thousand eight hundred and thirty-five were published in Venice, and only one hundred and forty-one in England. From its numerous printing presses issued the novels and poems which Shakespeare made such good use of in the construction of his plays, and which Ascham refers to as " the enchantments of Circes, brought out of Italie to marre men's manners in England." Readers of the time, says the same authority, " have in more reverence the triumphs of Petrarch than the Genesis of Moses. They make more account of Tullies' offices than St. Paule's epistles ; of a tale in Bocace than a storie of the Bible." To the varied attractions of Venice, its palaces, its festivities, and its silent highways, went the rich and gallant youth of England, to lounge and to study, to learn fencing, dancing, and singing. Rosalind undoubtedly refers to this custom of visiting Venice when she says to Jacques: "Farewell, Monseur Traveller. Look you lisp and wear strange suits; disable all the benefits of your own country ; be out of love with your nativity ; and almost chide God for making you that countenance that you are ; or I will scarce think you have swam in a gondola." Sir John Reresby, who was Member of Parliament for York, in the middle of the seventeenth century, writes in his diary, under date of 1656 : " I passed this winter there (Padua), and at Venice (where I went often) very pleasantly. The exercise I followed was chiefly music ; my studies were the language and the mathematics, for which science there was an admirable master, especially for fortification. I followed also fencing and dancing, but in quite a different method from that of France." The political influence of the Italian Republics upon this country was also considerable, as Mr. Lecky points out ; for he says: "A large proportion of the highest intellects acquired in Italy a knowledge of the Italian writers on government, and an admiration for the Italian constitutions, and especially that of Venice." Harrington's *Oceana*, published in Cromwell's time, bears many traces of this influence, and we have since improved our constitution in accordance with the principles there laid down. Harrington was the first English writer, I believe, who advocated the ballot. If Puritanism came to us from sober Germany, we caught the fire of liberty from the apparently frivolous Italian Republics. It was not Presbyterianism only, but with it a kind of intellectual Paganism, which made us tolerant and fond of freedom.

About the year 1587, William Shakespeare, a handsome, well-shaped man, with brown eyes and pensive benevolent face, twenty-four years of age, left Stratford for London, with a portion of the manuscript of *Venus and Adonis* in his pocket, and

perhaps some sonnets and imperfect plays. We have fixed upon
that year because Burbage, the tragedian, with whom we subse-
quently find him associated at the Blackfriars Theatre, visited
Stratford that year with the Queen's Players. Full of energy
and genius, and believing that "home-keeping youth has ever
homely wits," he went to London to make his way in the world.
Traditions about his own deer-stealing and his father's poverty
may be dismissed from our view. Burbage was a native of
Stratford, and there cannot be much doubt that he induced the
poet to seek a wider sphere for his gifts. Now, what was London like—his greatest view of the world—when Shakespeare
visited it for the first time? I take this to be the most important matter we have yet considered. London was a true mirror
of all the social and intellectual forces of the time; a gay, rich,
bustling, versatile city, in which a young man's mind would
quickly expand, and find something better to interest it than
"dead school-cram." As he trudges through Oxford and over
the Chiltern Hills to enter London by the New Gate, let us
briefly epitomise the national situation. The struggle against
the Papists was proceeding briskly; Robert Brown had com-
menced the foundations of Independency; Queen Mary had been
tried and executed; Newfoundland had been added to England;
Virginia had been discovered by Drake, and so named after the
Virgin Queen; he had beaten the Spaniards in the West Indies
and at Cadiz; Sir Philip Sidney had been killed at Zutphen;
the Armada was being got ready to conquer England; John
Fox, the martyrologist, had died; Marlowe had introduced blank
verse on the London stage in *Tamburlane the Great;* tobacco-
smoking was the last new fashion; and Queen Elizabeth had
issued her proclamation against the further growth of London,
setting forth that no more houses should be built within three
miles of its walls, and that only one family should inhabit each
house. You have probably seen plans of ancient London, and .
its gates, its narrow streets, its solitary bridge over the Thames,
its broad clear river, its churches, and its public buildings.
Islington, Holloway, Chelsea, Marylebone, and the Borough
were either fields or suburbs; Regent's Park was a tilting
ground; Spitalfields was an open grassy place; Smithfield was
planted with trees; Piccadilly was famous for its wild fox-
gloves; Cornhill market was surrounded by gardens; the no-
bility lived in the Strand and Drury Lane; and the prominent
buildings were the Tower, the Royal Exchange, Old St. Paul's,
and Wolsey's Palace at Whitehall. Though there were forty

thousand watermen living by work upon the Thames, it was a pleasant river; its banks adorned by gentlemen's villas, by stately trees, and Italian gardens. The city had a population of one hundred thousand souls, of whom some ten thousand were foreigners, engaged in various industries; Flemings, Frenchmen, Italians, Spaniards, and Portuguese, with here and there, by the riverside, a Greek, a negro, and a Turk. Here was an England in a single scope; here were hardy sailors and explorers, soldiers and buccaneers, trading merchants, politicians, lawyers, dramatists, artists. poets, satirists, gay cavaliers, and beautiful ladies, with their various costumes, characters, and places of resort. Here also were to be jostled against many of the lesser characters in Shakespeare's plays—tavern-hunters and swaggerers, garrulous citizens, witty rogues, needy usurers, pedantic parsons, running footmen, begging prisoners, ballad-singers, watchmen, pretentious apothecaries, quarrelsome dandies, and merry wives of Windsor. Shakespeare saw them all, and photographed them in his pages; mixing up town manners and country allusions; tempering the hot blasts of city licentiousness with flower-scented breezes from the rolling uplands of Warwickshire. You can discover he is not a town-bred poet by the sincerity of his love for nature and his familiarity with country life.

The narrow streets of London were constantly brightened by some pageant or other. " The paths," says Thornbury, " were filled by jostling serving-men, French pages and watermen, and wounded soldiers from the Dutch wars, Spanish gallants, Greek merchants; there were actors and bear-wards, masters of fence, bullies, and gentlemen-pensioners, and gay citizens' wives and *bona robas*, and falconers, all bright. coloured, shifting, motley, and picturesque. There was no dull monotony and stereotype of dress, face, and manners, but a never-ending variety, shifting and brilliant as the dyes of a kaleidoscope. There were beards of all classes and professions : the spruce, the pointed, the round, grey, black, and cream-coloured. All dress marked class ; the 'prentice passed with his round cap and truncheon ; the citizen with his trimmed gown and gold chain ; the noble with his silk cloak and scented doublet, gold spurs and spangled feather ; the needy adventurer with his rusty sword and greasy buff, or half Indian robe ; the scrivener with his rusty black coat and unfailing bag ; the divine with his cassock and his bands ; the yeoman with his unbarked staff ; and the court lady rolling by in her ponderous gilded coach. At Smithfield were the horsedealers; at St. Paul's the discarded servants and hungry spendthrifts; in Southwark the bull-baiters; at White-hall the courtiers; and at Westminster the lawyers. All the merchants were to be seen at a certain hour round Gresham in the Exchange, discussing the Muscovy trade, or the prospects of Virginia. The players at night met in The Mermaid or The Devil; the courtiers at the ordinaries, or at the promenade at St. Paul's, where politics and fashions were indifferently discussed. The life was more social and genial out of doors than now. Every man met his friend daily at St. Paul's, the theatre, the ordinary, or the court. The great men of the day were known to everybody, and could be heard talking at the tilt-yard or the pageant." The middle aisle of the old edifice of St. Paul's was the Prado of London. Twice daily, at eleven and three, did it fill with a motley crowd of young gallants, eager to display their new fineries; priests, soldiers, serving-men, newsmongers, pages, players, country visitors, and quick-fingered thieves. The choris-ters demanded spur-money of any one who entered with spurs on his boots. "And thus doth my middle aisle," says Decker, "shew like the Mediterranean Sea, in which as well the merchant hoysts sailes to purchase wealth honestly, as the rover to light upon prize unjustly. Thus am I like a common mart, where all the commodities (both the good and the bad) are to be bought and sold. Thus, whilst devotion kneels at her prayers, doth profanation walk under her nose, in contempt of religion." The taverns, too, were very numerous, and the resort of divers characters, who smoked down the nose—the common method then—whilst waiting for their ordinaries. After dinner, eaten without a fork—for "the laudable use of forks," as Ben Jon-son has it, did not come in until Shakespeare had left London and was living in comparative wealth at Stratford; after dinner, playing at cards and dice, powdering their talk with strange oaths, over their Bastard or Malmsey wine, and listening to narratives such as Hakluyt has recorded, of adventures on the sea, or fights with the Spaniards.

At night the streets were unlit, and very much at the mercy of thieves and roysterers of every description. Of course there were laws to restrain disorder, but they were easily evaded, and never very rigorously enforced. To blow a horn or a whistle in the streets after nine o'clock was an offence punishable by imprisonment. There were constant fights in the streets, how-ever, and the watchmen, who carried curved bills or halberts, a lantern, and sometimes a bell, were reinforced by the London apprentices, who sallied out whenever. the cry of " Clubs " was raised. " I'll call for clubs if you will not away," says the Mayor of London, in the *First Part of Henry V.*, when the partisans of the Duke of Gloucester and the Cardinal of Winchester are quarrelling. Perhaps nothing will more fully describe the whims of the watch than Dogberry's advice in *Much Ado About Nothing:*

Dogberry.—This is your charge : You shall comprehend all vagrom men ; you are to bid any man stand, in the Prince's name.

2nd Watch.—How if a' will not stand ?

Dogberry.—Why, then take no note of him. but let him go ; and presently call the rest of the watch together, and thank God you are rid of a knave.

Verges.—If he will not stand when he is bidden, he is none of the Prince's subjects. '

Dogberry.—True, and they are to meddle with none but the Prince's subjects. You shall also make no noise in the street ; for, for the watch to babble and talk is most tolerable and not to be endured.

2nd Watch.—We will rather sleep than talk ; we know what belongs to a watch.

Dogberry.—Why, you speak like an ancient and most quiet watchman, for I cannot see how sleeping should offend ; only have a care that your bills be not stolen. Well, you are to call at the ale houses, and bid them that are drunk get them to bed.

2nd Watch.—How if they will not ?

Dogberry.—Why, then let them alone till they are sober ; if they make you not then the better answer, say they are not the men you took them for.

2nd Watch.—Well, sir.

Dogberry.—If you meet a thief, you may suspect him, by virtue of your office, to be no true man ; and, for such kind of men, the less you meddle or make with them, why, the more is for your honesty.

2nd Watch.—If we know him to be a thief, shall we not lay hands on him.

Dogberry.—Truly, by your office you may ; but I think they that touch pitch will be defiled. The most peaceable way for you, if you do take a thief, is to let him show himself what he is, and steal out of your company.

I now pass on to describe the British Theatre in Shakespeare's time, as seen in the Metropolis. During the height of his career as an actor, a dramatist, and a theatre proprietor in London—for the Swan of Avon was all three, if he never held the horses upon which the gallants rode to the play, as some say he did—there were ten theatres in London, divided into two classes, public and private. The public theatres were, the Globe, in Southwark ; the Curtain, in Shoreditch ; the Red Bull, in St. John's Street ; and the Fortune, in Whitecross Street. The private theatres were Blackfriars, where Shakespeare played, and of which he

was part-proprietor, with Burbage and others; the Cockpit, in
Drury Lane; Whitefriars, on the Bankside; and three smaller
ones, the Swan, the Rose, and the Hope. Shakespeare's
plays were only performed at the Globe and Blackfriars, which
belonged to the same company of players. The distinctions
between the public and the private theatres were, in the main,
that the first were open to the sky in the centre, and the performances took place at or about two in the afternoon, and
chiefly in the summer; whereas, in the private theatres, every-
thing was architecturally much the same as in our day, candle-
light was used, and there were performances in the winter.
Plays were acted on Sundays as well as on other days, until the
year 1591; and at least two hundred persons, styling themselves
players, were living in the Metropolis. The Royal players wore
scarlet cloaks in public. The women parts were acted by boys,
and that fact, together with the absence of ladies of refinement
from the audience, will account for much of the coarseness of
many passages in Shakespeare's plays. The stage of the theatre
was ample, and strewn with green rushes; a fact which may
account for the " tragic-stride " with which modern play-goers
will be familiar. Boys let out stools at sixpence the time for the
dandies to sit upon at the sides of the stage, in full view of the
audience. Or these gay gentlemen sprawled full length on the
rushes, making notes in their tablets of witty passages for
use in conversation. Many of the quotations from Shakespeare,
which are a part of our common talk, were passed into use in
this fashion, before his plays were printed and published. If the
performance were dull, the dandies played cards, or smoked their
pipes, under the melancholy visage of Timon or Hamlet, and
in defiance alike of Ajax, Antony, or bluff King Hal. The
" groundlings," as they were called in the open theatres, the
pittites in the roofed ones, usually stood up during the performances, and were a disorderly, turbulent folk, whose behaviour
would not be tolerated for five minutes in a modern theatre.
The prices for admission were—one shilling to the boxes, sixpence
to the pit, and twopence to the galleries. The scenic arrange-
ments were primitive, very few painted scenes being used, and
labels, indicating the site of the scene, as " The Road to
Coventry," " A Port in Cyprus," and so on. The front scene
opened in the centre, and was drawn up from the side, not
rolled up. Nor was there much attention paid to correctness of
costume. Brutus and Cassius appeared in the Spanish cloak, and
were armed, in time of peace, contrary to the Roman custom.

A performance generally lasted about two hours, and at its close the players fell upon their knees to pray for their Sovereign. The " God Save the Queen," which sometimes figures at the bottom of our play-bills, is " a survival " of this custom. The wages of players varied from thirty to fifty shillings per week. Queen Elizabeth never visited any of the theatres, though she frequently had pieces played before her, and she is said to have suggested the *Merry Wives of Windsor*, in order to see Falstaff in love. Shakespeare himself played the Ghost in *Hamlet*, Adam in *As You Like It*, and the English Kings he so masterly portrayed. John Davies, referring to the last, says :

> Some say, good Will, which I in sport do sing,
>   Hadst thou not played some kingly parts in sport,
> Thou hadst been a companion for a king,
>   And been a king among the meaner sort.

The purpose of playing he has set forth in his own *Hamlet :*

> To hold, as 'twere, the mirror up to nature ; to show virtue her own feature, scorn her own image, and the very age and body of the time, his form and pressure.

Shakespeare's general civility and uprightness are mentioned by several contemporaries. Spenser styles him " pleasant Willy," and sings of his " gentle spirit." Ben Jonson calls him " gentle Shakespeare," " the applause, delight, and wonder of our stage." But the subtle critics, who discover autobiographic allusions in his sonnets, are full of mysterious intimations as to his moral backslidings. His sonnets, I may say, were circulated in MS. before publication, as Meres declares, and only eighteen of his thirty-six or seven authenticated plays were published during his lifetime. These were—*Titus Andronicus, Romeo and Juliet, Love's Labour Lost, A Midsummer Night's Dream, Much Ado About Nothing, The Merchant of Venice, King Lear, Troilus and Cressida, Pericles, Richard II., The First and Second Parts of Henry IV., Richard III., Hamlet, The Merry Wives of Windsor, Henry V.,* and *The Second and Third Parts of Henry VI.* The first collected edition of his plays was published in 1623, seven years after his death, from the prompter's books in use at the two theatres I have named ; a fact which will explain the disputes and contradictions, the ingenious emendations and audacious improvements of the hosts of critics who have explained and exploited him ever since. Owing to the non-publication of his plays as they were produced and acted, it was next to impossible that the purely literary student of the time should be able to form a fair estimate of the genius of the

man. It is not, therefore, at all surprising that we meet with
no references to him in the writings of Lord Bacon, in Sir
Thomas Browne, in Donne or Wotton, who may have been
unfamiliar with his more serious poems and plays, though he
had good patrons in Queen Elizabeth, in King James (who
wrote to him a letter of praise, which has been lost), in Lord
Essex, in Lord Pembroke, and the Earl of Southampton. He
was merely regarded as a popular player, and nobody suspected,
as Emerson finely puts it, " that he was the poet of the human
race." His fellow-townsman, Burbage, the tragedian, was of
greater repute ; and Tarleton, the jester, who sometimes appeared at the theatres between the acts of a play, was a
thousand times more popular, as abundant popular prints of him
attest. Sir Richard Baker, who was four years Shakespeare's
junior, and outlived him, wrote some Chronicles, of which he
himself says that, if all others were lost, his would be sufficient
to inform posterity. He makes the following reference to Shakespeare, which will illustrate what I have said. He has mentioned all the men of learning and note in Elizabeth's reign, and
then he says : " After such men it might be thought ridiculous
to speak of stage players, but, seeing excellency in the meanest
things deserves remembring, and Roscius, the comedian, is recorded in history with such commendation, it may be allowed in
us to do the like with some of our nation. Richard Burbage
and Edward Allen, two such actors as no age must ever look to
see the like ; and to make their comedies compleat, Richard
Tarleton, who, for the part called the clown's part, never had
his match, never will have. For writers of plays and such as
had been players themselves, William Shakespeare and Ben-
jamin Jonson have specially left their names recommended to
posterity."

This inability to obtain a proper perspective whilst Shakespeare was a living man, or but recently buried in Stratford
Church, accounts also for the disputes as to his subsequent life,
and for his companionship with Homer and Plato in having
scarcely any accurate biography. It was not until he had been
dead a century or two, until he had been dug up, as it were,
like an antique ruin, that his genius was fully appreciated ; that
he acted upon German literature like the spring sun upon frost-
bound wood and field ; and that Englishmen, everywhere, found
in him the most perfect poet of pathos, the richest humourist, the
subtlest drawer of character, the truest interpreter of ancient
history this world has ever yet produced.

Who were the contemporaries that overshadowed him? We have mentioned two or three, but there were many others. Amongst the dramatists there were mighty Marlowe, pathetic Webster, rugged Jonson, voluminous Decker, Marston, Massinger, and those " twin brothers in song," Beaumont and Fletcher. Amongst the poets proper Spenser stands first, the poet of chivalry, the sweetest of all songsters in the Elizabethan nest of singing-birds. His *Faerie Queen* became, it has been said, "the delight of every accomplished gentleman, the model of every poet, the solace of every soldier." After him came Chapman, the translator of Homer, " the proud full sail of whose great verse " Shakespeare himself praises in his sonnets ; Fulke Greville, the soldier-poet; Raleigh and Sidney, who Spenserised; Drayton, the rhyming chronicler; Daniel, the sonneteer ; Sackville, the allegorical. Amongst miscellaneous authors were quaint Roger Ascham, the philosophical Bacon, the prosing Camden, the learned Coke, the witty Donne, Fairfax, the translator of Tasso, deistical Lord Herbert of Cherbury, Holinshed the chronicler, the judicious Hooker, and the painstaking antiquaries, Speed, Spelman and Stowe. Of the men who competed with him by their deeds, there was a host. There was the brave Sir Humphrey Gilbert, whose dying speech should be the sailor's motto in all seas : " Courage, my friends ! we are as near heaven by sea as on the land." There was Raleigh, who discovered El Dorado, and by his tobacco, as some think, the fumes of another place ; there was the brave sealion, Sir John Hawkins ; there was Sir Francis Drake, under whose portrait in Plymouth Guildhall it is written : " The sunne himself cannot forget his fellow traveller ;" with a host of other naval heroes, whose brave deeds will never die. And who can forget Leicester, the Queen's favourite, " with whom England was too much occupied in his life time," says Froude ; Burleigh her Chancellor ; Bishop Jewel, the author of *The Apology* ; Archbishop Parker, who stripped our churches of their Papal ornaments ; or brave Peter Wentworth, who went twice to the Tower for speaking too freely about " the griefs of the Commonwealth," in the House of Commons ? Amidst such a galaxy. of stars, in the glare of so many cometary bodies, with meteors flashing across the heavens in bewildering splendour, is it any wonder that the dramatist, William Shakespeare, should have seemed a minor being, a man who frets his little hour upon the stage ; and that when his death had to be recorded in the Parish Register, at Stratford-on-Avon, there

should only be that detestable abbreviation "gent." put after
his name to mark the kind of man he was?

In the list of Shakespeare's rivals and compeers I have
omitted the greatest, Queen Elizabeth herself. The divinity
which is supposed to "hedge a King" transforms a Queen;
and accordingly the daughter of Anne Boleyn has been painted
as a moral monster and an angel of light, as an elaborate
dissembler, and simply as "Good Queen Bess." We should
remember the nature of her sex when we read the flatteries of
her courtiers. We should decline to see wholly with the
eyes of the lovers who dangled about her, or the enemies who
failed to conquer her, or the Puritans whom she disdained to
satisfy. She was vain beyond all precedent, it is said,
appearing in gorgeous dresses, which were like illuminated
editions of Æsop's Fables. She left three thousand silk dresses
behind her when she died. She envied the ladies who outshone her
in beauty and jewels, and she made great men remain on their
knees in conversation with her, as if she were a Saba or a
Semiramis. That she was naturally vain. I admit; but may
not the excess be attributed in part to the direct and indirect
flatteries of the time? Foreign potentates sought her hand.
Pope Pius V. thought her likely enough to bewitch Western
Europe unless subdued, not by courtship, but by conquest.
The poets were lavish in her praise. Shakespeare referred to
her in *Midsummer Night's Dream*, written when she was forty-two,
as "a fair vestal throned by the West," against whom Cupid
aimed his shaft in vain:

> And the Imperial Votaress passed on
> In maiden meditation, fancy free.

In her forty-ninth year, Raleigh, then in the Tower, wrote to
Cecil in a letter he hoped she might see, that he had been wont
to behold her "riding like Alexander, hunting like Diana, walk-
ing like Venus, sometimes singing like an angel, sometime
playing like Orpheus." "To see her was heaven, the lack of
her was hell," Hutton told her to her face. All the lesser
courtiers and poets chirruped in chorus the praise of the Virgin
Queen. You and I, superior as we may think ourselves to such
sickly adulation, would most likely be influenced by it; for it
takes a most heroic mortal to stand firm against much praise.
Under the pressure of her vanity. Elizabeth carried coquetry
to an excess not becoming either a pure vestal or a pattern
queen. But still it is not just to use to her the language of
Cardinal Allen, which I will not shock you by quoting entire,

when he urged the English people to "follow no more the broken fortunes of a mean and filthy woman." She had, it cannot be denied, the roughness of fibre which has been noticed in all the Tudors. She could hate terribly. She was often a most gifted dissembler. Her assent to the death of Mary Queen of Scots, and her quibbling both before and after the fact, sufficiently establish both points. She was self-willed beyond the range of ordinary mortals, wishing to do apparently impossible things. "As we track her through her tortuous mazes of lying and intrigue," says Mr. Green, in his *Short History of the English People*, "the sense of her greatness is almost lost in a sense of contempt." Yet, in sooth, she had many high qualities. She had lion-like courage, though it was frequently hidden under finessing irresolution. The envoy of Philip of Spain said she was "possessed by a hundred thousand devils." Upon one occasion she told the Bishop of St. Andrew's she was "more afraid of making a mistake in Latin than of the King of Spain, France, or Scotland." The Pope excommunicated her, but she did not flinch a hair's breadth ; Philip sent an Armada against her, and this is how she addressed her troops at Tilbury : "I know I have but the body of a weak and feeble woman, but I have the heart of a king, and of a King of England too." Elizabeth was a clever woman of business, and displayed great tact in selecting ministers and managing the House of Commons. Unlike the Stuarts and the Bourbons, she knew how to yield gracefully. She really loved the English people and the Protestant religion. "I have desired," she said, in one of her many pulse-stirring addresses, "to have the obedience of my subjects by love, and not compulsion." In another she says : "Never has a prince loved his subjects more than I do ; and no jewel, no treasure, no happiness of any kind can counterbalance the value of this affection. Nor do I wish to live any longer than while my government is for the advantage of all." The speech just quoted is one made in 1601, in yielding to the petition of the Commons to abolish the monopolies for trading in certain goods and to certain ports, which she had bestowed upon her favourites, or sold to pushing merchants. She had been careless of English interests in this matter, though her actions were strictly in accord with the customs of the Crown. But she compensated for her largesses to her nobles by great cautiousness in taxing the common people, whose poverty had been marked in the early part of her reign. Burleigh had taught her that the Treasury was not her own money, but committed to her for the safety of the people and the good of her country, and she practised what he taught her only too well, starving alike the army and the fleet. The annual cost of the navy was but £4,000, equal to £8,000 of our money. At the present moment it would barely pay the salaries of our admirals, and yet we do not always consider ourselves safe from invasion. The ships which put to sea from Plymouth to attack the Armada were short of provisions, short of gunpowder, and only too well provided with sour beer. The largest sum she ever drew from the people in one year was £280,000. It was to be an exceptional sum, but when she found the people could comfortably pay it, like more modern governors, she did not reduce it.

If we look at her various legislative acts, we shall say she attempted too much rather than too little. A Commissioner, who was sent to examine into the working of some of her enactments in the country, wrote to Burleigh, her Secretary : " Sir, would to God ye would not meddle so much as ye do, nor be so earnest." Elizabeth had more than our current faith in an Act of Parliament. She had beggars whipped under them until their backs were bloody. She put tramping scholars of the same ilk into the pillory. She tried to curb undue luxury by law, and to promote English trade by altering the diet of the people. She set herself the task of thwarting the economic tendencies of the age by regulating wages, which were low enough in all conscience (from twopence to sixpence a day), and by amending the land-laws. Wealthy franklins from the towns were buying up small farms, and turning the arable into pasture for the sake of sheep and their wool. She insisted upon these sheep-farms being broken up ; she forbad the exportation of sheep ; she enacted that every cottage should have four acres of land attached to it, under severe penalties. Of course, she failed to effect any important changes. The " good yeomen," whom Henry V. is made to address before Harfleur, " whose limbs were made in England," and who had shown " the mettle of their pasture" in many a sturdy fight, were beginning to disappear. Farm-labourers, hired by the day, were also beginning to take the place of the labourers who used to live in the farm-houses, and take their meals below the salt at the common table. Foreign trade was growing in British hands, but agriculture was declining. Indeed, it is difficult to find an age, now or in the past, when British agriculture was not only declining, but about to die. But it never dies ; it suffers a transmigration of souls—I had almost said, soils. The old common-lands were being enclosed, to the detriment of the poor, though to the improvement of the land. Unenclosed land was rented at about sixpence, newly enclosed land at eightpence and ninepence per acre; ordinary farms at from two shillings and sixpence to three shillings and sixpence. Shakespeare resented this enclosuring. He was not " able to bear " the intended enclosure of Welcombe Common, near Stratford, we are told. No enactments prevented enclosures elsewhere, however, and the Queen's mind was not specially moved to the subject. But she was not indifferent to the wants of the common people. She reformed the coinage, restoring the tester from twopence-halfpenny and fourpence-halfpenny to sixpence. She founded public schools at Westminster, Harrow, and Rugby. Above all, she established the system of English Poor-law, upon the main lines on which it exists at the present day, by ordering public workhouses to be built, and contributions to be levied from each parish in their support. The power of the Crown was much greater then than it is now; but Elizabeth did not greatly abuse it to the damage of her people. She conferred votes upon thirty-two towns during her reign, and her forty-five years of rule were, on the whole, years of growing prosperity, of internal tranquillity, and sleepless devotion to the public weal. She found England poor, dejected, tormented, humiliated; she left it proud, powerful, prosperous, and unconquered. Cranmer's prophecies in Shakespeare's *Henry VIII.* had been fulfilled.

> She shall be lov'd and fear'd : Her own shall bless her :
> Her foes shake like a field of beaten corn
> And hang their heads with sorrow : Good grows with her :
> In her days every man shall eat in safety
> Under his own vine, what he plants ; and sing
> The merry songs of peace to all his neighbours.

My task is nearly done. I have said little about Shakespeare himself, and the range covered by his works, and despite what I have said about his time, it may still be as great a mystery as ever how he could have written the plays and poems which have made his fame ; his genius may remain the final something which cannot be accounted for. I have nothing to say as to the reign of James I., which Shakespeare lived to see, for the simple reason that it was either a continuation or a caricature of the reign of Queen Elizabeth.· Whatever made the Elizabethan age is of importance in the understanding of Shakespeare; it is not for me to follow out its gaiety until it became the profligacy of the Stuarts, or to show how its Protestantism flowered into

C

the Puritanism of Cromwell, or how its personal loyalty to the
Sovereign, and its growth of liberty among the common people,
ended in a conflict between the kingly prerogative and the rights
of Parliament. These are matters of ordinary history; and we
must take a final glance at the Elizabethan people. I have
described their manners and customs; their lives and amusements;
from which you will have inferred their general character. Let
me sum it up, in a few brief words. In the time in which
Shakespeare lived, as well as in the comedies and dramas
which he wrote, we cannot fail to notice a gaiety of spirit, a
freedom of manners, a terseness of language, a ripening of
intellect, a sensual energy, a consciousness of power, and a love
of enterprise, adventure, and political freedom, which have been
continued to the present day. The Elizabethans, as M. Taine
says, had new senses given to them, and they were untroubled by
theories. Hamlet, the metaphysician, is also Hamlet the irre-
solute, the half madman, in Shakespeare's conception of him.
The superstitions of the time were yielding to the intellectual
stimulus derived from Italy; the discovery of the New World
gave them a wider horizon; the growth of riches brought
leisure for cultivation; the printing press increased the studies
of the scholarly, whilst the drama expanded the faculties of
the ignorant; a fresh uprising of what was best in Paganism
braced their minds with science, and fortified their bodies with
physical training. An Englishman's courage was never doubted
the wide world over. Frenchmen said we were " as savage as
our own mastiffs; " the Italians thought us " wild beasts; " it
was only the Spaniards who said the Elizabethans were weak
and cowardly, and that was before the Armada. The morals of
the Elizabethans were none of the best, I am afraid. Swearing,
drinking, gaming, and cruel sports were wofully common. James
I., you know, paid a bigger salary to the man who had charge of
his fighting cocks, than he did to his principal Secretaries of
State. Duels and street brawls were of constant occurrence;
highway robberies and murders were generally undetected; and
bad characters of all kinds were extremely common. An excess
of coarse energy strikes us everywhere. But there were not
wanting the better elements of the chivalry Spenser described in
his romances and allegories. Men of letters were a power in the
land; newspapers, fluttering forth feebly after the Armada defeat,
were beginning to be a flock; the pulpit was free; science was
dawning; and some of the superabundant vigour of the people
found vent in colonisation and geographical discovery. Political

parties, as they now exist amongst us, were coming into being; our maritime development received its plenary impulse; and our position as a European Power was incontestably settled. In short, the age of Elizabeth, the age of Shakespeare, fixed our language in its present form, and set " the text of modern life and modern manners." " We must be *free or die* who speak the tongue that Shakespeare spake," says Wordsworth. It was poor George III., in his ignorant scorn, who asked, " Was there ever such stuff as Shakespeare?" It is to Shakespeare, however, that we owe the glorification of the age in which he lived, the reflection of its vices, the record of its virtues, the embodiment of its intellect. We have not yet got beyond his sayings, his probings, his pathos, his passion, his colossal conceptions—they are parts of an imperishable inheritance. He has made us proud of the name and style of Englishmen, proud of living, working, and dying for

> This royal throne of kings, this sceptred isle,
> This earth of majesty, this seat of Mars ;
> This other Eden, demi Paradise ;
> This fortress built by nature for herself.
> * * * * *
> This happy breed of men, this little world,
> This precious stone set in the silver sea.
> * * * * * *
> This blessed plot, this earth, this realm, this England.

—— If in your memories dwell
A thought which once was his, if on ye swell
A single recollection, not in vain
He wore his sandal shoon and scallop-shell.

BYRON's Childe Harold.

[*Reprinted from* SHARPE'S LONDON MAGAZINE, *January*, 1861.]

A PILGRIMAGE
TO STRATFORD-ON-AVON.

A PILGRIM myself, I can readily pardon the enthusiasm of ancient palmers, wandering to sacred shrines to erase from their lives the sins of the past, and imbue them with a saintlier holiness. Carp at it as one may, there is something of a hearty sentiment beneath it all. We are still human, if we have discarded staff, wallet, and scallop-shell. We are always placing ourselves beneath certain influences, real or suppository, and hoping to catch inspiring airs after the same mediæval manner. At Mecca, why should we not be Mahometized? in Cappadocia, why may we not expect to imbibe the dragon-killing vigour of Saint George? and in Stratford-on-Avon, what doth hinder that we, too, should not become writers of sonnets and dramas? All our ruin-visiting, our place-worshipping, our " Murray "-in-hand galloping abroad, has something of this ancientness about it. Whenever we can, we place ourselves hopefully in the matrix of some kingly soul, and our pigmy glance wanders round, while vanity whispers to us, " Go to ; why should not we also be famous?"

I stay not, after such an apologetic preamble, to refer to my own feelings in the matter. I made my pilgrimage with whatsoever intention was uppermost ; I think there was reverence in it. Here are the notes ; as for the rest, see ye to it.

The morning train from Coventry to Warwick fills with the usual collection of business and pleasure travellers; and, taking our seats, we are soon whirled through shrub-planted cuttings, with here and there a primrose peering through the delicate green of newly-tressed pines, whilst occasional long sweeps of country

opening to the view, besprent with flocks, relieve the dulness of
an April morning. Suddenly we are startled from our pastoral
reveries, by a stout porter's voice bawling out, " Kenilworth "—
awakening dim remembrances of Leicester, Amy Robsart, and
old Mervyn, and photographing on the mind a picture of ivied
ruin. The Castle, however, is a mile distant, and hidden by a
clump of trees. All we can see is part of the straggling town,
with rows of houses spreading out like the combs manufactured
by the inhabitants. A snort and a plunge, and we are off again,
and soon all eyes are turned to the river Avon as we cross it, for
the first time realizing our propinquity to the great poet's birth-
place. Alighting at the station, which serves from its equi-
distance for both Warwick and Leamington, a walk of some two
or three hundred yards brings us to the Avon, with its quiet
waters reflecting the pollard-willows on either side; and its
green pleasure-boats swaying lazily to and fro, like the slug-
gard, whose voice still complains in song. The epithet Keats
applies to this river one can now fully understand. In its
quiet flow, and serene surface, with a sort of lonely witching
influence about it, well might this fanciful poet ask :

> Did ye never cluster round
> Delicious Avon, with a mournful sound,
> And weep?

The first impressions Warwick gives are pleasing ones. An
old Grammar-school, built of stone, and looking as crabbed as the
severest of pedagogues, and a tree impaled by the roadside, are
appropriate introductions to the old city. On every side a philo-
sophising spirit may observe an evident struggle between old and
new forms—a rich and venerable past contending manfully with
a plain but gigantic present. Every street is brimful of lessons
and homilies, and a modern Yankee and a thirteen century man
might each find matter for contemplation and sober conversation.
Passing the " Spade and Pick-axe," a sign sacred to the memory
of the first clown in the fifth act of " Hamlet, " who sings

> A pick-axe and a spade—a spade !

and where I am reminded by my companion that henceforth to
quote anyone else but Shakespeare will entitle me to the stocks,
we are in a street leading down beneath the castle-keep, which is
the last strong hold of bygone days. Some enterprising individual has run up a row of modern houses, with painted pane-
work on the front to match the rest ; and these, with a few
smaller houses, are all that are modern in this quiet street. At
the bottom of it the view is a magnificent one. Here the Avon

spreads itself out triangularly, feeding a water-wheel and running over the falls. The pillars of an old stone bridge, covered with ivy, cross one of its arms, and huge trees all round, robed in the same greenery, fling their shadows athwart the water, and sway in their branches the nests of cawing rooks. A solitary chestnut tree shakes its white catkins above the water, and, grey and grim, the donjon-keep looks down upon us with imperial pride. We cannot resist a little reverie. A voice as of an ancient grey-beard breaks on our ears, and the massive pile looks at its image in the river, while it holds converse with the ancient houses in the streets, and both exult in their strength and age, and laugh, goblin-wise, at those mean, flimsy, contract-built houses. A third voice now stirs the air dolefully, and we can recognise the modulations of the tones. Hark! " *Mis-er-ere— Dom-ine!*"

Leaving behind us the castle, with its memorials of the famous Sir Guy, of Warwick—the huge punch-bowl, the terrible lance, and the giant armour—we thread the aristocratic streets, admiring their several beauties as we pass; here a fine old mansion with armorial griffins carved in oak above the portico, and further on a quaint-looking hospital for poor men, founded by Dudley, Earl of Leicester, as we are informed by a Latin inscription over the gateway. We reach the highroad between Warwick and Stratford, with eight miles before us, and a prospect of rain from sundry jagged and sullen clouds rising up from the horizon. A few heavy drops descend upon us; but, inculcating upon my companion the philosophy of a stout resistance, and of a determination to enjoy a thorough wetting as essentials in securing immunity from the angry heavens, we set forward manfully along our way.

About a mile from Warwick is Longbridge turnpike-house, which must not be passed by unnoticed. This house is indeed one of the prettiest of the kind we have ever seen. A carved gable-end fronts the road, and there is an artistic oaken porch over the door. The framework of the windows is also of oak, and adorned with exquisitely carved and laughing Sileni, whose curls unite over the window, and whose beards twine away beneath like serpent-rings. Honeysuckle, woodbine, or clematis (emulating around the porch these fantastic rings) were alone wanting to complete this admirable picture. By the roadside here and there are huge white-painted iron pumps, doubtless used in some way for draining or irrigation, but irresistibly connected in one's mind, spite of their modern air, with the giant form of the

famous Sir Guy, and seemingly used to quench the immense
thirst, or fill the small vat of this imbibing Briton. Further on
our way, a bowlegged brewer's drayman, who seemed to have
passed his whole life astride a cask, attracted our attention, and
an examination of his barrels showing a portrait of the great
bard affixed to each one near the bung, the well-known lines
suggested themselves : " As thus : Alexander died, Alexander
was buried, Alexander returneth unto dust ; the dust is earth ;
of earth we make loam : and why of that loam, whereto he
was converted, might they not stop a beer-barrel?" Shakespeare's
curse, however, would have turned all the beer sour in his case ;
and I myself can vouch for the prime mellowness and stingo of
the Stratford Brewery's " best."

The scenery in Warwickshire is eminently rich and wooded.
Short gnarled oaks, the remnants of primeval forests, appear on
every hand, and green rolling sand-slopes stretch for miles, with
waving corn and grass.   It was the month the great poet himself calls " proud-pied April," and every nook and bank was
covered with violets, enabling us to comprehend the frequency
with which he draws images from them, accusing this " sweet
thief" of having stolen his love's breath, and dyed her veins with
its purple pride.   Here, too, in rich clusters the cowslip droops
her delicate head, as when Ariel slept within her bell.   We are
in the very centre and store-house of Shakespearian imagery, and
our conception is increased by the scenery around us ; not bleak,
barren, nor gorgeous ; but rich, calm, and varied in aspect, with
an indefinite primeval quaintness about it, at once charming and
suggestive.   There are no cloudy eminences, whence all the tints
of the landscape blend into haze, and the scenery is extended,
but diminutive ; each view is a near-lying picture, an harmonious
semblance of passive and active life.   Yonder are the Edge Hills,
with their memories of Cavalier and Roundhead ; that of Bar
Beacon, near Birmingham, whence British and Roman bale-fires
have leapt in flames ; and nearer at hand are the thick-leafy groves
of Charlecote, the shallow brawling brook and deep and peaceful
river.   A mile or two over Black Hill, and bosomed in the valley,
the thin spire of Stratford Church fixes our wandering gaze ;
whilst the river, conspicuous by its row of pollard willows on
either side, which had never been very distant, now comes closer
up to the highway, winding about like the fabulous sea-serpent.
It now commences raining, deluding not only ourselves, but creation generally it would seem.   Daises are only half-folded, lambs
still skip in the meadows, and larks go up aloft, having evidently

with us made the most erroneous meteorological observations, and determined to be jolly notwithstanding.

The entry into Stratford is very modern. A row of clean genteel houses with modern pointed roofs introduces you to the main street. To your left is the memorable stone bridge of fourteen arches, built—so Sir Richard Baker tells us in his Chronicle, than which I know few quainter—by Sir Hugh Clopton in the seventh year of Henry the Seventh's reign, he being then Lord Mayor of London. Partly destroyed in the Parliamentary war, it was re-built in 1652, and has since undergone some improvements. A turn to our right, and we are in one of the main streets of the town; broad, open, and well-studded with shops and inns. Here in particular we see the Red Horse, where Washington Irving stayed on his memorable visit. The rain comes down thick and fast, but cannot quench our glowing enthusiasm. One's eyes run on before, galloping up every ancient house-front for the well-known signs. I forbore to ask my companion, who had been here more than once, as to the locality of the house we were making for, wishing to discover it myself, and receive a vivid impression. At last, we get into a narrower street, and are confronted by a very ancient house. This cannot be it; but he may have looked on it many times in passing, and a pathetic melancholy prevails in its aspect.

The veritable house is at length before us. Standing back from the rest, with its nearest end new-beamed by the committee, who have pulled down the contiguous houses, to restore it to its original form as it stood in the fields, an angular sign records, in dingy yellow letters, that " the Immortal Shakspeare was born in this house." The window of the bottom room, used in the late Mrs. Hornby's husband's days to exhibit butchers' meat, is now filled with a pane of ground glass, and the whole house exteriorly has that black grim look which books have, when they have survived the ups and downs and thumbings of centuries. The room once used as a shop has lost the stains upon the floor formerly noticeable by travellers, but its slabs of slate are broken and worn by the feet of pilgrims. Its whitewashed walls are covered with strange names and verses, and its sunken chimney corners give to the imagination the vision of a boy Shakespeare, in the jambs by the fire. The second room on the ground-floor is a larger one, and has the fire-place to your left immediately you enter. And here we behold a sad memorial of curious bickering in the shape of a board, which reads thus :

" About the year 1810, Lucien Buonaparte, brother of Napo-

leon, passing through Stratford, visited this house, and inscribed
where this frame now hangs four lines in honour of the poet.
These, the then owner of the house, a silly and capricious person,
ordered to be whitewashed over. As they are the composition
of one of the most distinguished foreigners who have done
homage to Shakespeare, a copy is here subjoined : *

> 'The eye of genius glistens to admire
> How memory hails the sound of Shakespeare's lyre.
> One tear I'll shed, to form a crystal shrine,
> Of all that's grand, immortal and divine.' "

This silly and capricious person was no less an individual than the
garrulous frosty-faced Mrs. Hornby, who, pretending to a portion
of Shakespearian inspiration, both by descent and locality, wrote
grotesque tragedies and poems. When she was ejected from the
house, she had all the walls whitewashed over, but fortunately
without any glue in the liquid, so that most of it was easily
brushed off again.

Looking on the right hand wall as you pass to the stairs, you
observe the neat signature of Harriet Beecher Stowe, already
dim and indistinct. A dozen or so broad oaken and worm-eaten
stairs lead you to the chambers. You ascend and turn into the
left, and from an opposite corner is a bust you know full well,
looking calmly at you from out its dim shadows. All is at first
disenchantment and disillusion, a melting of waxen wings, and a
coming down with a thump and thud against the solid common
earth. It is impossible at first to realize that so great a man
was born in so humble a chamber, and you listen to the remarks
of the cicerone with a sort of dubious delight, a kind of " I
would it were all true." But that dubiousness will subside. Go
into the shadows of that dim corner, face-to-face with that
eloquent bust, lay your hand on that manly brow, and fill your
mind with a living form and soul like his, and the thickly written
walls shall gradually possess an irresistible witchery. Run over
the names. On the low window opposite the door are the diamond-
written ones of Sir Walter Scott and his friend Lockhart ; on
the ceiling above, the neat autograph of Thackeray ; on the
chimney to the left, in entering, is the dashing signature of
Emerson ; and at the one corner, but undistinguishable, those of
Washington Irving and Lord Byron. By the side of the fire-
place is a list of actors, foremost in which you recognise the

---

*As a singular coincidence I may mention that deeply-carved on one of
the topmost stones in Mervyn's tower at Kenilworth, and almost worn
illegible, is the name of Jerome Buonaparte. There is no date.

round hand-writing of Edmund Kean, the father of the present actor. There are also observable the names of G. G. Norman, Thomas Brindley, G. V. Brooke, J. C. Pope, and Eliza Vestris. Here are the names of enthusiastic Germans, forgetting their Goëthe and Schiller, and there of those volatile Frenchmen, equally oblivious to Corneille and Racine; here a soldier, and there a clergyman some after-comer has denominated the "gibbet-parson;" names written in drooping womanly lines, in bold manly dash, in boyish fulness, and in clerk-like firmness and precision. A verse here and there attracts your attention, the writers hovering unsteadily between the sublime and the ridiculous. One says :

> Thy praise, O Shakespeare, vain the attempt to write,
> Till angel minds with mortal pens unite.

Another does not forget himself ; but is anxious to leave an echo behind :

> Would I, great bard, like thee to thoughts
>   Sublime were given,
> And could with words of fire the mind
>   Exalt to Heaven !
> But since no pen can do thee justice but thine own,
>   I'll simply write—
>   Ventriloquist James Flemington.

Again, as a climax :

> Though Shakespeare's bones (?) in *this here* place do lie,
> Yet *that there* fame of his shall never die.

You pore amongst the books lying about to find what the room was years gone by, whilst its interest and reality are visibly deepening. The light illumines a thousand names, until they glimmer strangely and half-phosphorescently, and a meditative mood falls upon you, like a twilight veil. The source of the Nile and the centre of the earth, are nothing to this world-omphalos. The dim outflowing and the broad inflowing tides lap around, and you seem to stand in what Carlyle calls "the conflux of the eternities." Here, in this dim low room, was born a power which has radiated to the ends of the earth, interpreting alike the silence of primeval forests, and the mystery of magic islands in the sea ; speaking audibly amidst the ruined palaces of Carnac, and the whirling streets of London. Blind thought gropes for an analogy, and finds in the rays of the sun, reflected in the flaunting tulip, the rich rhododendron, the delicate hyacinth, the enamelled rose, and the modest violet, and in all the flowers that mimic the colours of morn, and noon, and even, the aptest illustration of that mind which has inspired so many others, and brought them here, in silent eloquence, to own his wisdom and power and their gratitude and veneration. Our reverie is at length broken by the melancholy drip and patter of the rain upon the window, and, after a stay of two hours or more, we thread our way towards the Church of the Holy Trinity.

A sign over a house we pass upon our way informs us that certain relics are exhibited there; but having no inclination to fritter away our enthusiasm upon the stock of the identical matchlock with which young Shakespeare shot the deer, his tobacco-box, Toledo blade, spy-glass, and other things, we do not yield to the temptation. Three very interesting memorials are passed in proceeding to the church. First, there is the Tuscan Town Hall, with a figure of the poet, in a niche, in front, leaning upon a pillar, and pointing to a scroll inscribed with the lines commencing :

The poet's eye in a fine frenzy rolling.

Within this hall, the first year of its erection, the memorable Jubilee was held in 1769. Next we come upon the Chapel of the Guild of Holy Cross, a fine old building, with much of its Gothic beauty rendered more conspicuous by age. Above the clock in the tower the sign of the Cross still exists, in all its quaint and venerable suggestiveness. It was ancient in Shakespeare's time, having been built in 1443. Contiguous to this, and of plain and modest exterior, is the Town Guildhall, built in the thirteenth century, and originally possessed by the same fraternity. It consists of two long rooms, each rich with associations of our bard. In the lesser one the business of the Corporation is generally transacted. Here, as High-Bailiff, in 1568, having previously passed through the offices of court-leet juryman, aletaster, burgess, constable, and chamberlain, and in 1571 as chief alderman, the father of the poet sat in full civic dignity. In this room, also, Shakespeare probably saw his first theatrical entertainment. It was customary for the companies of players (mostly noblemen's servants) to go through their first performance before the chief dignitary of the town, and there are entries in the Stratford Borough accounts for payments to players during Master John Shakespeare's official term. The end of the room seems conveniently elevated for a stage, and has a small room at hand for a tiring-room. Here the youthful poet no doubt saw, in 1579 (being then about sixteen), the performance of " my Lord Strange's men," on the 11th of February, for which five shillings was paid, " at the commandement of Mr. Bayliffe;" and in the same year the " Countys of Essex plears,"

for which was awarded the liberal sum of fourteen shillings and
sixpence. In the next year the Earl of Derby's players were
paid eight shillings and fourpence for their performance. In
this hall, too, an entry was made in the Town Books, in 1579, of
the election of William Smythe and Richard Courte, to supersede
Mr. John Wheeler and the poet's father; "for that Mr. Wheeler
doth desyer to be put out of the companye, and Mr. Shaxspere
doth not come to the hall when they be warned, nor hath not
done of long tyme."

The upper room of this building is the Grammar-school, where,
as a *grammaticus*, under the instructions of Thomas Hunt and
Thomas Jenkins, the young Shakespeare must have greedily
imbibed not only "a little Latin and less Greek," but a great
deal more than we wot of, with all our rummaging amongst
possible and impossible authors.

The aspect of the church is a pleasant one. The tower has
the appearance of great age, and is reported to be coeval with
the Norman Conquest; while the mixed Norman and Saxon
styles indicate it to have been built upon the site, and with part
of the materials of the old Saxon monastery, standing in the time
of St. Egwin, third bishop of Worcester. Its graveyard is quiet
and solemn, and with the Avon murmuring a mellow dirge by its
side. An avenue of fine limes leads up to the porch; and, once
within the grim old walls, the reverie broken in his birth-
chamber is resumed. We have exulted in his fame and univer-
sality, and now we must be hushed and humbled to learn, even
from him, life's last sad and sorrowful lesson. We had deemed
him before exhaled around us, like a Narcissus; but every echo-
ing footfall and every monument proclaims a truth we cannot
escape from.

Our attention is first called to the Clopton monuments. An
uninscribed tomb is supposed to be that of the famous Sir Hugh
Clopton; and on a second one are the recumbent effigies of
William Clopton, Esq., and Anne his wife. Above them, in the
wall, are the bas-reliefs of their children; one or two of them
swathed and bound, to denote their death in infancy. A third
monument, beneath an arch, is that of George Carew, Earl of
Totnes, Master of Ordnance in Queen Elizabeth's time, and Joyce,
his Countess, daughter of William and Anne Clopton. Over
them all is suspended a rusty and dinted helmet, and the rotten
tattered remains of some gay banner that once perhaps streamed
before the gaze of the warrior-queen herself. There is a legend
which records that during the sweating-sickness, in some un-

known period, when the Clopton vault was opened to admit a
second victim to its virulence, the form of the first one (that of
a fair golden-tressed girl in her grave-clothes) was found drooping against the wall, but seemingly asleep. The glimmer of the
torch, however, revealed a small wound she had bitten in her
own white shoulder, and the fact that she was dead, and had
been buried alive. A dusty, cobwebby room is still shown in
Clopton Hall, said to have belonged to this fair-haired but unfor-
tunate Charlotte. However such a legend might have disposed
me to have remained in piteous contemplation in this chapel had
the sexton told it us, as I did not hear it until afterwards, I
passed impatiently onwards to the chancel.

The marble bust of the bard looks from its niche of black
marble Corinthian pillars, above the front of the altar-railing
over the remains of himself, his wife, and "wittie Mistress Hall."
A pen is in his right hand, and his left rests on a scroll upon
which he is supposed to be writing those grand lines of *Prospero's:*

The cloud-capp'd towers, the gorgeous palaces.

The countenance is calm and thoughtful, the lips slightly parted,
the elevation of the whole above the spectator giving the open
brow more height and massiveness. A close-fitting doublet enve-
lopes his broad chest like a cuirass. When coloured, to represent
life, the eyes were hazel, the hair and beard of a fine auburn.
Sculptured about seven years after his death, it may be regarded
as representing him in the prime of life, a few years prior to his
decease, although it has not the repose of age about it visible in
the Earl of Ellesmere's Chandos picture. As I stood underneath
it, I ran over, mentally, all the portraits I had seen of him, and
all their phases were traceable in his countenance. There was
that of Martin Droeshout's famous print, with its horse-shoe
collar and contemplative cast ; also that of Wivell, and the one
prefixed to the 1640 edition of the Poems—all seemingly taken
one from the other. The head is bald, but more cliff-like than in
his bust ; the hair is long and lanky, and the upper lids drop lan-
guidly over the dreamy eyes. A slight moustache and imperial
adorn the lips ; and the broad and rather massive chin is well
thrown out by the large and rather awkward-looking collar.
The countenance is that of an amiable and intelligent youth of
about twenty-five ; and from this, one can easily go back and
imagine that of the ingenuous school-boy, emerging from his
father's house, or sitting amongst his companions in that long
upper-room. The second class of portraits picture him in about
his thirty-fifth year—I mean the Roubiliac bust and the designs

taken therefrom. He there approaches nearest the human ideal
of manly and vigorous intelligence. A slight beard curls from
his chin; his eyes have lost their languor, and beam softly
bright; and his whole aspect is kingly and inspired. The words
of Aubrey are upon my tongue : " He was a handsome, well-
shap't man ;" and we can easily believe the sequel, that he was
" very good company, and of a very ready and smooth witt."
The third series of portraits—as the picture of Cornelius Jansen,
the Chandos picture, and the one in the possession of Mr. Charles
Knight—are much later ones. A sweet serene aspect pervades
them all ; but, in aiming at repose, the lofty forehead that marked
the earlier pictures is lost in the general breadth. Looking up-
wards to his niche, and passing before me these visions, I seemed
to have secured a newer and more human interest in his life and
works, and to see him as he moved and mused in that retirement
and fellowship with nature so congenial to his mind, not long ere
he lay beneath that heavy slab.

Of the inscriptions underneath the bust, the Latin one is much
to be preferred, and may be roughly translated thus :

> He had the wisdom of Nestor, the wit of Socrates, and the
> polish of Virgil.
> The earth hides him ; the people mourn him ; Olympus has him.

The other, however, must be given, although it does no one
credit :

> Stay, Passenger ! Why goest thou by so fast ?
> Read, if thou canst, whom envious Death has plast
> Within this monument—Shakspeare, with whom
> Quick nature dide ; whose name doth deck y^s tombe
> Far more than cost ; sich all y^t he hath writ
> Leaves living art but page to save his wit.
> Obiit Ano. Doi. 1616, ætatis 63, die 23 Ap.

A plain sandstone slab, with the memorable exhortation and curse
written across the middle, rests above his remains. The stones
of his wife and daughter, besides him, are of slate, with a much
primmer and preciser look about them. Beneath the niche, I
should also mention, is the door of the *carnerie*, or chancel-house,
into which loose bones were cast, and to the propinquity of which
many attribute the poet's curse. This, of course, makes him the
selector of his own burial-place. The monument to my "Johnny
o'Combe," and the gorgeous chancel-window, representing scenes
in the life of Christ, are passed over with very little interest, and
we shape our course to the vestry, to write our names. The
sexton we find has prepared a rough index to his book, whereby
the names of several living celebrities are seen at a glance. An

ancient brass-embossed Bible, with its steel altar-chain attached,
also lies upon the table. Its interior is imperfect; but its bind-
ing will stand for centuries to come. An engraved brass-plate
on the cover reads :

William Wrighte & John Noble,
Churchwardens for ye Borough.
Stephen Borman & Rich. Gibes,
Churchwardens for yᵒ Parish.
Anno Dom. 1695.

In the parish register I find the entry of the poet's baptism, in
the Court-hand of the period :

"1564.
April 26. Gulielmus filius Johannes Shakspere."

This, however, is not the original entry. About 1600, orders
were issued for the better preservation of parish registers, which,
up to then, had been kept in loose leaves ; and as the whole
character is in the same hand, up and subsequent to that time,
it has evidently been copied from a more ancient one. I did not
stay to look at the baptismal entries of his children, or the sorrowful one that records the death of his little son Hamnet,
but passed to that of his own burial—and plain and common-
place enough it seemed to read :

"1616.
April 23. Wm. Shakspere, Gent."

I closed the volume with a sweet sense of pleasure that his closing
days were spent in placid ease and rural retirement, with the
dignity of well-won honours to surround his noble brow. I
rejoiced, too, as an Englishman, that I could pay him the modest
tribute of a passionate pilgrim.

The clouds still shook down upon us their tears, as, emerging
from the church (our ramble back by Charlecote now impossible),
we sought refreshment in one of the many inns with which
Stratford abounds. An eight miles trudge in the drizzling rain
and dark might have been enough to have discomfited the most
enthusiastic pilgrim ; but, as the train rattled towards Coventry,
I still stood in that humble room and above that sacred dust, and
only when the bustle of arrival had shaken me, and Peeping Tom
was looking waggishly down upon me from his corner, did I
return to surrounding things.

JOHNSON AND TESSEYMAN, PRINTERS, YORK.